BILLY GRAHAM

Sam Wellman

Illustrated by
Ken Save

BARBOUR
PUBLISHING, INC.
Uhrichsville, Ohio

ISBN 1-57748-103-8

Published by Barbour Publishing, Inc.
       P.O. Box 719
       Uhrichsville, Ohio 44683
       http://www.barbourbooks.com

Member of the
Evangelical Christian
Publishers Association

Printed in the United States of America.

1

Every morning long before the sun came up, Billy trudged to the barn with his father to milk cows. It was 1924, and Billy was nearly six years old. He could already milk a cow almost as fast as a man could. It was a good thing, too, because his father, Frank, owned over twenty milk cows. Folks around Charlotte, North Carolina, bought a lot of milk from his father's dairy.

"Seems mighty peculiar the way cows fill up with milk again so fast, Daddy," said Billy in the darkness of the barn, thinking about milking the cows again that afternoon.

"It's the Lord's blessing," said his father.

"Sure enough is, sir," agreed Billy quickly. He quit talking.

Billy knew when to be quiet—most of the time. His daddy could yank him off his milking stool and whop him on the bottom before Billy knew what had happened. It seemed his daddy had six hands to get all that done so fast. His daddy didn't get mad or anything. He just grabbed Billy like he grabbed a squawking hen for Sunday dinner and did what he had to do. And his daddy never blinked an eye.

"It's real pleasant in the barn, Daddy," volunteered Billy. The air was sweet with the smell of hay and milk and cows. He got along fine with the cows. He liked them. And they liked him. One cow stepped on his foot once. But that was a pure accident.

After milking, Billy got to go outside and feed the chickens and the goats. He liked chickens. But, oh, those wonderful goats! He liked them so much. And they liked him. Goats were just about the warmest, smartest, funniest critters on earth. And so friendly.

After Billy finished his chores, he washed up and

"IT'S REAL PLEASANT IN THE BARN, DADDY."

sat down to eat a breakfast of grapefruit, eggs, sausage, grits, toast, and chocolate milk. He heard his mother say, "Maybe today will be the day when the Lord comes again." She said that every morning. There was deep longing in her voice.

"Yes, ma'am," mumbled Billy as he wiped milk off his mouth.

His mother asked, "Do you remember Proverbs 3:5-6 that I taught you?"

"Trust in the Lord with all thine heart; and lean not unto thine own understanding. In all thy ways acknowledge him, and he shall direct thy paths."

"That's just fine, Billy," said his mother.

"Isn't this the time of year we pull up the sweet potatoes, Daddy?" asked Billy.

"It's September and that's the right time of the year to pull sweet potatoes, but you're going to be in school," answered his father.

"School! When?" blurted Billy.

"TRUST IN THE LORD WITH ALL THINE HEART..."

"Today," said his mother. She looked worried.

"Today?" cried Billy.

"Go get your good clothes on," said his father. "You've seen the school bus go by our farm a hundred times. You even wave at the bus driver. Well, today you get to ride that bus."

Billy liked the bus driver. He liked just about everybody. In fact, now that he thought about it, he did like everybody. And it was a fact that just about everybody liked Billy. Was there anybody who didn't just about melt when Billy grinned ear to ear? Billy dressed quickly and sat in the living room, fretting over school. He had never been to school before. He could hear his parents talking in the kitchen. Their voices were warm and friendly.

"Billy's going to be tall and lean like you, Frank," said his mother.

"But he's got your blonde hair, Morrow," said Billy's father. "And by dogs if he doesn't have his

HE HAD NEVER BEEN TO SCHOOL BEFORE.

granddaddy Crook Graham's eyes! Those blue eyes could stare right through a plate of lead."

"Granddaddy Crook Graham was mighty ornery." His mother's voice was worried now. "How do you think Billy will do in school?"

"He doesn't seem to ever get tired ." His father's deep voice was weary. "Has that boy been eating sweets?"

"Nothing more than an apple or a pear," said Billy's mother quickly.

Billy's skin crawled as he listened. Suzie the cook kept a jar of candies on the back porch. So Billy and his younger sister Catherine ate a lot of sweets. Oh God, please don't let Suzie get in trouble, Billy prayed. Billy liked Suzie so much. And she liked Billy.

"Billy will start school in a few minutes, and everybody in Mecklenburg County will know about him then," groaned his father.

"HE DOESN'T SEEM TO EVER GET TIRED."

"We won't let the devil win," said his mother. "We'll pray and pray and pray."

"But Billy pushed a dresser out of an upstairs bedroom into the hall and plumb down the stairs," said his father. "You saw him at the top of the stairs. He just grinned at you like a puppy dog. And out in the hen house he overturned a basket of eggs."

"He knocks dishes off the center of the table," sighed his mother.

"I didn't know that!" snapped Billy's father. "He's going to get a good whipping for that."

Billy fumed as he listened. Didn't his mother already whip him for that? She got out that switch of hers and really whopped him. He was sure of it. But he was too smart to complain. That only made Daddy lay it on heavier. Billy would just grin. That worked about as well as anything.

"Let us pray Billy is going to outgrow this rebellion," added Billy's mother. "Oh, how we must pray."

"I DIDN'T KNOW THAT!"

The Grahams prayed a lot. Billy's mother had said from memory many times, " Love the Lord thy God with all thine heart, and with all thy soul, and with all thy might. And these words, which I command thee this day, shall be in thine heart: And thou shalt teach them diligently unto thy children, and shalt talk of them when thou sittest in thine house ."

Billy peeked into the kitchen. Tears ran down his father's cheeks. Arms raised toward the ceiling, his father prayed in a trembling voice, "Oh, Lord, help a wayward child."

How his father could pray!

That night when Billy returned on the school bus to the Graham farmhouse, his mother rushed out of the house. "How was your first day of school, Billy?" she asked anxiously.

"I don't think the teacher likes me," answered Billy.

"HOW WAS YOUR FIRST DAY OF SCHOOL, BILLY?"

"Oh no! What did you do, Billy?" His mother's eyes looked around the farm as if searching for Billy's father.

"I didn't do anything." And he wasn't going to do anything at school either. Not after his daddy talked to him before Billy left that morning on the bus. If Billy ever wanted to play with his gang of goats or play baseball or play Tarzan or ever do anything fun again, he'd better not get in trouble at school. And his daddy's eyes hadn't blinked once.

"But why doesn't the teacher like you?" asked his mother, interrupting Billy's thoughts.

"I don't know." The truth was Billy had been so afraid of getting in trouble he forgot to smile. He was dressed as smart as if he was going to Sunday school, but he forgot to smile. And the teacher didn't even know he was alive.

"You take her a little bouquet of flowers tomorrow," suggested his mother.

"I DON'T KNOW."

"I don't know how." And Billy went inside to change into his work clothes. On his way to the barn, a flock of bleats and purrs and whimpers collected behind him. Say, that would make a great trick, thought Billy. He would teach his flock of goats and dogs and cats to trail behind him as he rode his bike. He would practice and practice. He had to use his time better at home. Because grade school sure wasn't going to be any fun.

The next morning after chores and breakfast, Billy rushed outside to ride his bike. Before the school bus appeared, he had his flock trailing behind him. He rode up and down the gravel road in front of the house. Several cars honked at him in delight. He grinned and waved. What a great trick!

But there came the bus. He waved to the driver, then rode back and forth a while. Finally the bus driver wasn't laughing anymore. Billy dumped his bike.

"YOU TAKE HER A LITTLE BOUQUET
OF FLOWERS TOMORROW."

As he got on the bus, Billy's mother handed him a small bouquet of flowers. "Now you give these to your teacher," she said.

Billy got off the bus at the one-story brick school building surrounded by a wasteland of dirt packed down by flying feet. He walked right past frowning kids into the school and handed the bouquet to the teacher. This time he didn't forget to grin.

"For me?" She saw him for the first time. "What a sunshiny smile! What's your name, boy?"

"Billy Graham, ma'am."

"BILLY GRAHAM, MA'AM."

"ME!" HIS GRANDMOTHER LAUGHED.

2

Every day from then on was just bursting with school and work and fun. Billy never got tired. Yet when he went to bed, he was asleep so fast he couldn't remember trying to fall asleep.

On Saturdays, Daddy might drive him and Catherine the eight miles over to the farm of Grandma Coffey. There they played in her orchard under long rows of sagging plum and pear and apple trees.

Then Grandma Coffey sat them down to milk and cookies. She told them about Granddaddy Ben Coffey who fought at Gettysburg during the Civil War way back in 1863 and lost his eye and his leg. Then he came back to marry Lucindy Robinson.

"Who?" gasped Billy.

"Me!" his grandmother laughed.

Sometimes Grandma Coffey would tell Billy and Catherine about the days when Billy was born. "One fall day in 1918 your mother had picked butterbeans, then started having a baby that night. It was not until late afternoon the next day, November 7, that you were born, Billy, kicking your legs like a wild frog."

"Did they have to tie a rope to my legs and yank me out?"

"No. Folks don't pull stubborn babies out like they pull out stubborn calves."

Billy was like a different boy in school. His parents couldn't believe it, given the wild way he acted at home, but he was. He hardly said a word in class.

But one second off the school bus in the afternoon and Billy felt so good he would run around behind the bus and turn off its gas valve. Pretty soon the bus would sputter to a stop, and the driver would hop out to stare Billy down. Billy would just grin,

"DID THEY HAVE TO TIE A ROPE
TO MY LEGS AND YANK ME OUT?"

and no matter how hard the driver tried to be mad, he couldn't keep from grinning himself.

"It's such great fun being back on the farm again," said Billy. "Even if I do have to do chores and play with Melvin." For Billy now had a baby brother Melvin, nearly six years younger.

When Billy reached the age of ten, he got to hang around his daddy and Uncle Simon. The two men talked about the gospel—the good news about Jesus —that was told in the Bible.

That was when Billy really learned how hard his daddy worried about his soul. Had his daddy used his life as God wanted? And was he really saved?

His daddy fretting like that began to worry Billy a little. Billy just figured folks went to church and once in a while tried to remember God's words in the Bible so they knew how to behave, and that was that. A person could pretty much plan on a one-way trip to heaven and eternal glory, whatever that was. But

HAD HIS DADDY USED HIS LIFE AS GOD WANTED?

all this worrying by Daddy worried Billy.

And the Scripture from Ecclesiastes that Mother made Billy memorize began to make sense: "Remember now thy Creator in the days of thy youth, while the evil days come not ."

"Sooner or later the Scripture is always proved right," she said, "because it is truly the Word of God."

Billy's daddy built a new two-story brick home with white pillars, landscaped in front with oaks and cedars. It even had water and electricity and inside toilets. Billy's corner bedroom faced a wall of trees behind the house. The room was perfect, except for Melvin snoring in one of the two iron-framed beds.

The dairy was doing very well with its red barns trimmed in white. The farm now had fifty dairy cows, more every day it seemed.

Billy loved baseball like no other game. He loved to pound his fist into the stiffness of a brand new glove. He loved to swing the bat, to hear the loud

BILLY LOVED BASEBALL LIKE NO OTHER GAME.

whack, to see the flight of the ball. Those moments were all sweeter than chocolate cake. Once in a while his bat launched that rare comet that soared so high and so far that playing Major League Baseball seemed possible some day.

One day Billy couldn't believe his ears when he heard who was coming to Charlotte. "Babe Ruth?" he gasped. "The player who hit sixty home runs in just one season?"

"Yes," Daddy explained, "the Babe is barnstorming between seasons."

And the day came that Billy saw Babe Ruth swing a monstrous bat and blur a baseball into the heavens over Charlotte. If that wasn't enough, Daddy took him up to shake the hand of the moon-faced giant.

"Hi ya, kid," rumbled the Babe as he roughed up Billy's hair.

Also at the age of ten, Billy went on a reading binge. He nibbled his fingernails to the quick as he read

'HI YA, KID," RUMBLED THE BABE.

books about Tarzan. Acting out the books was fun, too. Deep in a thicket, Billy climbed high on the branches of trees to perch above. What fun it was to observe his bewildered "chimp" Melvin looking for him.

Billy's mother was bewildered, too. "How can you read books all the time, Billy, but not get good grades in school?"

"School doesn't give a test on Tarzan," joked sister Catherine.

Billy managed to get B's and C's and D's. His father just grunted at his report card unless it showed a poor grade in behavior. Then the belt came out. But Billy's mother was upset by C's and D's. Billy soothed her by picking bouquets for her every Sunday.

Billy and his mother were very close. Even after he went to high school, he would tell Mother about the girls he thought he liked. And he discussed himself, too. He had been studying the mirror for some time. If being the tallest, thinnest kid in his

"SCHOOL DOESN'T GIVE A TEST ON TARZAN."

class wasn't bad enough, his eyes were sinking right back into his head—deeper every year. Lately they had darkened around the edges, so they seemed to be peering out of a cave.

"And my nose and chin jut out fantastically like they do in those Mother Goose characters," Billy fretted.

Mother reassured him. "Are you worried? A boy with your wavy blond hair and your strong features and your heavenly smile?"

Billy always could fall back on his smile. It did seem like kids warmed up to his smile. So why worry? The girls seemed to like him. He was more relaxed in school now. Once in a while he spoke up in class. It wasn't so much fear that kept him from talking, as it was he had nothing to say.

Now if they had a course on baseball, he would be a regular chatterbox. He was sure of it, although when he had to give an oral report in English class

THE GIRLS SEEMED TO LIKE HIM.

on a book about baseball, he slouched and mumbled and fumbled for words. His dangly hands groped for a place to hide.

But the older Billy got, the more sure of himself he became. He began to act at school like he acted at home. Love just bubbled out of him. The girls really did like him. And he liked them.

He could have pulled away from his family at this time, feeling more and more comfortable at school. But his family didn't let him. Just because he wore white shirts and bright painted ties and ice-cream slacks and a winning smile to school didn't mean he got out of chores or meals or prayers after supper at home.

The Grahams stayed close, and Billy played with his sister Jean—even though he was fourteen years older. It was a good thing he was anchored in his family because about this time a lot of things happened in his life. And with the good came the bad.

LOVE JUST BUBBLED OUT OF HIM.

"FOLKS ARE CALLING THIS THE GREAT DEPRESSION."

3

One day Billy knew something bad had happened. Billy's father never said more than a few words, except when he prayed after supper, but he was grumpier than usual. So Billy asked his mother, "What happened?"

"We lost all our money at the bank. Everybody did. Folks are calling this the 'Great Depression'. Some kids may have to drop out of school to go to work. But not you, Billy. We have four hundred regular customers. Folks with kids won't give up their milk, and most of them will keep paying us. And besides, what did the Lord tell us in Luke 12?"

"Watch out! Be on your guard against all kinds of greed; a man's life does not consist in the abundance of his processions."

"Perfect," she said, pleased.

Then his father had an accident. A hired hand had been sawing a plank of wood with a circular saw and a knot flew off like a cannon ball, striking Frank in the face. From the nose down his face was smashed in. All his front teeth were gone and that was not the worst of his injuries. At the hospital he lapsed into a fight with death.

Billy's mother comforted the children, "Don't you remember your father saying the Lord 'is my refuge and my fortress, my God, in whom I trust' from Psalm 91?"

A few years before, Billy had been right there when Grandma Coffey, about eighty, rose up from her sick bed to cry out that she saw glory's blinding light and the outstretched arms of Jesus. She even saw angels and her dear departed Ben. Then she fell back on the pillow and died!

"She saw the Lord Jesus and heaven," someone

"SHE SAW THE LORD JESUS AND HEAVEN."

said in awe.

Billy knew Jesus and heaven were real. How could folks worship and pray and obey all their lives and think otherwise? Still, he was amazed. Grandma Coffey's death seemed to connect him to the other world, the paradise he couldn't see. He was so thankful to Grandma Coffey. He did not fear death. And he trusted God.

Billy's father recovered, his sad face even more woeful. But inside he had changed.

One morning Billy was amazed to see dozens of folks parking cars by the farmhouse as he left for school. The men from the club were gathering right in Frank Graham's pasture by a pine grove. They were going to pray all day long.

Their wives were walking to the house to spend the day praying with Mother. And they were all still there when Billy came home after school to start his chores.

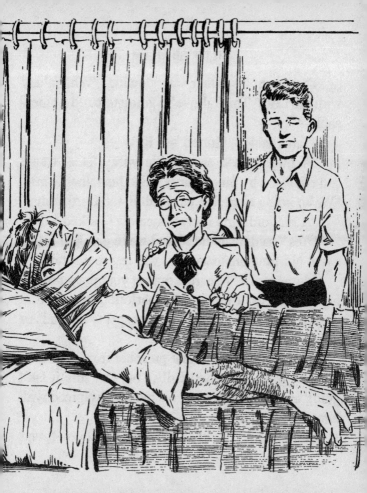

BILLY'S DAD LAPSED INTO A FIGHT WITH DEATH

That night his father was glowing. "What a day with the Lord! This fall we're going to build a tabernacle—"

"Tabernacle!" blurted out Billy.

"A huge house of worship with a steel frame and enclosed by pine boards," said his father firmly. "We're going to revive our faith in the Lord Jesus."

"A real old-time revival meeting?" asked Billy.

"Yes," said his father. "And we're going to get us a real old-time preacher who will revive our faith!"

Mother said, "I heard a man at your prayer meeting begged the Lord to let Charlotte give rise to a preacher who would spread the gospel to the ends of the earth!"

"I don't know who that preacher from Charlotte is going to be," laughed Billy, "but I'm sure it isn't going to be me." Not even his mother disagreed with him.

Billy was driving the family car to school. It was

"WE'RE GOING TO REVIVE OUR FAITH IN THE LORD JESUS."

amazing how sporty the dark blue Plymouth sedan became when the driver had a nice tan face, wavy blond hair, and a dazzling smile. His interest in girls had advanced beyond talk. But doing more than kissing a girl outside of marriage was just unthinkable.

Billy reminded himself constantly with Scripture: "God is faithful, who will not suffer you to be tempted above that ye are able; but will with the temptation also make a way to escape, that ye may be able to bear it."

And God was faithful to Billy.

So Billy had two great interests: girls and baseball. He was sure he was a natural-born first baseman, with windmill arms that snapped balls out of the air like a bullfrog snapped flies. It was just a matter of time before he started connecting with the bat.

Milking cows had given him a grip that could make a grown man cry. And his long, farm-strong arms blurred the bat when he swung. If he hit the ball

BILLY HAD TWO GREAT INTERESTS: GIRLS AND BASEBALL.

square, the ball soared into the sky. The problem was that he never hit it square, except in batting practice.

"You'll whack it someday," encouraged Melvin.

Mordecai Ham came to Charlotte late in the fall of 1934 to preach at the revival meetings Billy's father had talked about. But how would Billy find time to go? He was back in high school starting his junior year, and when he wasn't working on the farm, he played baseball. Or he talked to girls. But when Billy heard Mordecai Ham said the kids at the high schools in Charlotte were sinful, he found the time.

"I've got to hear this Dr. Ham for myself," Billy complained angrily. "Somebody's got to stand up for the honor of Charlotte's young people."

Billy went to the revival with Albert McMakin, a young man who had been in the tabernacle in downtown Charlotte before. The tabernacle built by the Christian Men's Club stunned Billy. He seemed transported into paradise. The immense interior was

"I'VE GOT TO HEAR THIS DR. HAM FOR MYSELF."

lit by dozens of high-swinging bulbs as sunny as angels. The air smelled of delicious pine from the sawdust that covered the ground. Hundreds of folks were already there, sitting on benches and crates and chairs. And there was room for many more.

"I want to be right down front," insisted Billy sticking his pointed chin farther out.

"No, you don't," said Albert in such a forceful way that Billy didn't argue.

So they sat in one of the back rows. "I could never understand why folks sit at the back," grumbled Billy.

He really couldn't understand. Scared as he was when he first started school, he had sat down in the front row—silent, but all ears and eyes. Billy gawked around. "How many folks are coming, Albert?"

"Four thousand most nights."

The tabernacle slowly filled. Billy had never felt like he did that night. The tabernacle was a pulsing,

" I WANT TO BE RIGHT DOWN FRONT."

living thing. There were so many people. And they seemed so eager to hear the Word of the Lord. Were folks so thirsty for the living water?

Mordecai Ham appeared on the stage. He was about fifty years old, with a thin white mustache and only a fringe of white hair above his ears. He wore rimless glasses on a pasty white face.

Billy was disappointed. How was this colorless man going to take on a crowd of four thousand? Billy sat up tall so he wouldn't miss anything. He hoped the colorless Mordecai Ham spoke loud enough. Would this insignificant preacher dare repeat his slurs against the students at the Charlotte high schools?

As Billy watched, Mordecai Ham's pale face grew redder. "You are a sinner!" bellowed Mordecai Ham. He pointed right at Billy!

"Me?" gasped Billy. He slumped in his chair. How did Mordecai Ham know about him chasing girls? Mordecai Ham preached on and on about sin.

HE POINTED RIGHT AT BILLY!

Before the evening was over, Billy really knew he was a sinner. How ignorant he had been about revivalists. Mordecai Ham had thrashed Billy and 3,999 other souls from the tops of their heads to their toenails!

Billy went back to the meetings again and again. He had never heard and seen anyone who could preach like Mordecai Ham. He had heard some pretty good preachers over the radio. But in person, with all his senses tuned in, this preaching shook Billy's soul.

But Billy made sure he never sat in Mordecai Ham's line of fire again. He joined the choir, which stood behind the preacher. He was next to a boy his same age, Grady Wilson.

Grady liked to tease. "Billy, you sing worse than a calf bawling for its mama."

Billy did not care if Grady Wilson knew he couldn't sing or not. He was not going to be the target of Mordecai Ham again.

Every night Mordecai Ham ended his preaching

HE WAS NEXT TO A BOY HIS SAME AGE, GRADY WILSON.

by calling folks to the altar to accept Jesus as their Savior and be born again.

One night after Mordecai Ham invited sinners to the altar, Billy felt the presence of the living Christ. Was Jesus telling him to go to the altar? Billy resisted. He was already a Christian. He was baptized. Of course he didn't remember being baptized. He was just a baby. But he was Christian. Wasn't he?

Billy glanced at Grady Wilson. Grady was very troubled. "I thought I was already saved," he stammered. "Maybe I'm not." Grady lurched forward to the altar.

What if Billy's own soul wasn't saved? Would he wait until it was too late to be saved?

BILLY FELT THE PRESENCE OF THE LIVING CHRIST.

"I'M A CHANGED BOY."

4

Billy found himself stumbling awkwardly to the altar. Then his father was suddenly beside Billy, tears in his eyes. Sad-faced Daddy had wanted Billy to be born again all along and never once pestered him about it. God would make it happen or not happen. And God made it happen.

"I'm a changed boy," Billy told his mother that evening.

But in his bedroom later that night, to the sound of Melvin snoring, Billy felt all his flaws magnified. He wanted to feel righteous, but he felt like a great sinner. Maybe he didn't really understand what living in Christ meant.

Weeks later, his mother said, "You've calmed down, Billy. I know you have always loved other people, but you didn't slow down long enough to let them know it."

Billy had changed. He was very conscious of sin. And not everyone appreciated it. He'd started meddling with kids at school, telling them right out if they did something wrong. So he stopped.

But some kids started calling Billy and Grady Wilson the Preacher Boys, anyway. And they were not teasing. Billy was learning that some folks wanted their religion watered down or not at all. If it reminded them of their sins, they became very angry.

"Blessed am I when people persecute me because of Jesus," Billy reminded himself. "That's what the Bible says." But it hurt deep inside because Billy liked everyone. And it was very hard to pray for persecutors like the Bible said. But he did.

Billy began preaching to the children on the farm. Once Billy had dreamed of being lord of the jungle like Tarzan. Later he'd dreamed of playing baseball in

HE WAS VERY CONSCIOUS OF SIN.

the Major Leagues like Babe Ruth. Now he dreamed of mastering thousands of sinners under a big tent. "Come down and be saved," he would cry, and thousands flocked to the altar—in his imagination.

I wonder if I could really do that? he asked himself. He remembered how poorly he gave oral reports in school.

Then he heard Grady Wilson was going to preach inside a real church! Grady was just a senior in high school like Billy. Billy went to listen.

Before the sermon, Grady asked Billy, "Can you loan me your watch, buddy? I've got to be careful, so I allow enough time for my whole sermon."

Billy loaned Grady his watch and sat down in a pew with Grady's girlfriend. He was amazed when Grady began preaching. Grady was really good. Billy thought, That's my buddy Grady up there. Plain as mud. Why can't I do that, too?

All during the sermon, Grady's eyes darted down

GRADY WAS REALLY GOOD.

at Billy's watch, and he kept winding the stem. He had to make sure the watch kept running. After the sermon, Grady handed Billy his watch. "I'm sorry about the watch, buddy. But you shouldn't have held hands with my girl. It made me kind of anxious."

Billy just had to laugh. Grady always made him laugh. Besides, he was so amazed that Grady could preach he didn't even mind that Grady had wound the stem right off his watch. If plain-as-mud Grady could preach, why couldn't Billy?

On the farm, the family started talking about Billy becoming a preacher, too. "Maybe Billy will be that preacher from Charlotte who spreads the gospel to the ends of the world," said Mother.

"God willing." Billy's father looked pained to presume such a thing.

"Grady Wilson is going out west to Tennessee to that Bible college run by Dr. Bob Jones," volunteered Billy.

GRADY ALWAYS MADE HIM LAUGH.

"I never heard of it," said Mother.

"What's it cost?" asked his father.

"Well now, you know Grady couldn't afford much, Daddy."

"That's it, then. It's Bob Jones," said his father, looking like he could make no better bargain than that.

Suddenly Billy was out of high school with a diploma in his hand. Albert McMakin had left Charlotte to sell Fuller brushes door to door in South Carolina. He invited Billy to come and sell brushes with him that summer. Grady Wilson would join them too.

"But I thought you were going to help me on the farm this summer," said Billy's father.

"I can save up money for college this way, Daddy," gushed Billy.

"Don't worry, Frank. He'll be back in two weeks," scoffed an onlooker.

BILLY WAS OUT OF HIGH SCHOOL WITH A DIPLOMA.

On that discouraging note, Billy left with Grady Wilson to go to South Carolina. The very first time Billy tried selling, he opened his case of brushes, found one of his cheapest Fuller brushes, and knocked on the door of his potential customer. The door opened. An exasperated face appeared in the doorway. "Yes?"

"I'm Billy Graham, ma'am. Your Fuller Brush man. I'd like to give you a free brush today." He held out the brush. "All you have to—"

"Thanks, sonny." The woman snatched the brush out of his hands and slammed the door.

"Say, wait just a cotton-picking minute!" Billy stared at the solid door. He never even got a chance to smile.

He learned fast. At the next house, Billy said the same words, smiling pure sunshine. But he took his sweet time digging though hair brushes and tooth-brushes and clothes brushes for the free brush.

"SAY, WAIT JUST A COTTON-PICKING MINUTE!"

Never again did a customer get a free brush without hearing an unstoppable avalanche of words. And Billy made sure his customer was blinded by his smile.

Like everything Billy did outside of school, he threw himself into it heart and soul. He really did believe his brushes were the best in the world and no housewife could survive without them. He began to sell brushes left and right. And only later when he stopped to think about it was he amazed, because while he was selling, he never doubted for a moment he was going to sell every brush in his case.

Albert McMakin was amazed too. "You're selling more brushes than I am, Billy."

After a few weeks, Billy was making as much money as a man with a real job. But he didn't save much of it. Billy liked nice clothes, and he bought himself suits and hand-painted ties. And of course a salesman needed several pairs of comfortable shoes

BILLY LIKED NICE CLOTHES.

—nice saddle-top shoes, too, not clogs. One thing was for sure. At the end of summer, Billy would have a mighty fine wardrobe.

One Sunday afternoon in Monroe, North Carolina, a preacher-friend named Jimmy Johnson took Billy and Grady Wilson to a jail. Facing cells full of grumbling prisoners, most of whom were recovering from a wild Saturday night, Jimmy suddenly pointed at Billy. "I have a young fellow here who was just recently saved. Give our friends your testimony, Billy."

Billy was so surprised he dropped his case full of brushes. He froze. Preaching terrified him. He began to nervously wring his yellow-trimmed green suit coat he had taken off because the jail was so hot and sticky.

Jimmy was amused. It was an old trick on would-be preachers.

Help me, Lord, prayed Billy. Hadn't he practiced

HELP ME, LORD, PRAYED BILLY.

a hundred million times? Get me started, Lord, he prayed.

"I'm glad to see so many of you came out to hear me today," said Billy, remembering. He heard Grady cackle with glee. Billy screamed, "I was a sinner!" He was talking to God now. Did he hear a weak "Amen" drift from a cell?

"I was no good!" He punched the air. "I forgot God!" Another weak "Amen, brother" seemed to drift out of a dark, sweltering cell.

Billy began to walk around and punch the air with his suit coat as he spat out his testimony in short sentences. "I didn't care about God! I didn't care about people!" He hunched over, then shot straight up with each sentence. Always the arms flailed.

"Finally I accepted Jesus!" His voice bounced off the walls, each word as loud and clear as a church bell. A few more "Amens" made him louder yet. "Jesus brought me joy!"

BILLY BEGAN TO WALK AROUND AND PUNCH THE AIR.

How long he talked, Billy didn't know. He could hear "Amens" roll out of the cells after every sentence. The prisoners were responding! He felt like he could fly. Finally he stopped, trembling, in a state of joy he had never felt before. It would be a good while before the excitement wore off.

"So that's what preaching is really like," he gushed to Grady later. And Grady seemed amazed by what Billy had done.

"SO THAT'S WHAT PREACHING IS REALLY LIKE."

"THANKS, BUDDY," SAID PRESIDENT GRADY WILSON.

5

After summer was over, Billy's father drove the boys out west to Bob Jones' Bible college in Tennessee. Billy had a plan to get himself and Grady elected officers in the freshman class. Billy nominated Grady for president of the class. Grady won the election. But when it came time for Grady to nominate Billy for an office, they found out officers couldn't nominate candidates.

"Thanks, buddy," said President Grady Wilson afterward, as innocent as an angel. "The first part of your plan was brilliant."

Billy got even at the talent show. He talked Grady into singing a duet. Grady frowned. "Are you sure? I don't want to hurt your feelings, but you sing worse than a lovesick hound dog, Billy."

As Grady stood up after being announced to sing, he suddenly realized he was standing alone. He managed to croak through the song as Billy hunkered down in his seat.

When a fuming Grady returned to his seat, Billy tried to look as innocent as an angel. "You were right. I don't sing well enough. Thanks for sharing your wisdom with me, buddy, before it was too late."

After a few weeks, Billy was unhappy because of the strict rules at the college. Boys couldn't talk to girls. Every letter in or out was read by school officials. For the first time in Billy's life, he had trouble sleeping.

When he returned home for Christmas vacation, everyone thought Billy had the flu because he was so miserable. He had to be dragged along in his father's new green Plymouth when the Grahams drove south to visit his mother's sister in Florida. But at each gasoline stop as they drove deeper into Florida, Billy

BILLY WAS UNHAPPY BECAUSE OF
THE STRICT RULES AT THE COLLEGE.

began to be the first one out of the car.

"So this is Florida," he muttered and gawked. "It's warm for December."

By the time they neared Orlando, he was leaping from the car. "Look at the palm trees!" His arms spread out. "Look. Flowers everywhere!" He flailed his arms. "Feel that balmy air." He punched the air. "Can this be December?" He clapped his hands. "What a paradise!"

After they visited Billy's aunt in Orlando, the Graham family took a side trip. Near Tampa, in the midst of orange groves, the Grahams stopped to survey the Florida Bible Institute.

Pale stucco buildings with red-tiled roofs overlooked tennis courts and a sprawling golf course. Nearby, the Hillsboro River crept along under cypress trees with moss hanging from their limbs.

"It's beautiful," gushed Billy.

His mother said casually, "It's a fine institution

"IT'S BEAUTIFUL," GUSHED BILLY.

to study God's Word. I read about it in Moody Monthly." Then Billy recalled hearing about this Florida school before. How grateful he was to his mother. He daydreamed of striding across campus in bright sunshine, glowing in his lime-colored suit and hot pink tie, free to talk to any pretty girl he saw.

Two months later, Billy's father drove him back to the Florida Bible Institute. Billy's only regret was that Grady couldn't afford the school.

Billy soon learned many preachers—or evangelists—came to vacation and lecture there because the institute maintained part of the hotel for that very purpose. Students carried luggage, caddied golf, waited tables, washed dishes, and met veteran evangelists.

Billy drank in their lectures. He sat wide-eyed and gulped down their informal discussions, too. One name kept emerging as a giant: Billy Sunday.

Billy Sunday had been everything Billy Graham wanted to be. He had been a Major League Baseball

BILLY DRANK IN THEIR LECTURES.

player. At the age of 28, he'd had his best season ever with 123 hits and 84 stolen bases—the most stolen bases in one season until Ty Cobb topped the record many years later. Sunday was paid more in one month than most men made in one year. And suddenly he quit baseball to evangelize for Christ!

Old evangelists explained how Billy Sunday used the pulpit like a stage actor, with a leather-lunged voice and exaggerated gestures to capture the farthest listener. He stomped his feet and pounded his fists. He raced across the platform and slid like he was sliding into a base. He screamed at "bull-necked, hog-jowled, weasel-eyed, sponge-spined, mush-fisted, yellow-livered, hell-bound sinners."

"How could anybody ever top Billy Sunday?" asked Billy Graham.

The warning was out at the institute: a student had to be ready to preach at all times. Billy polished four sermons until he had what he figured to be at

"HOW COULD ANYBODY EVER TOP BILLY SUNDAY?"

least two hours of preaching in his heart. Who knew when he would be called?

John Minder, a dean at the school and the director of the Tampa Gospel Tabernacle, took Billy with him on Easter vacation to Jacksonville. And sure enough, Billy got his call: he was going to preach that very night in Bostwick, a small town near Jacksonville!

About thirty people were in the congregation that night. Billy got wound up and hammered out all four sermons in less than ten minutes. The experienced Dean Minder easily filled in the remaining time. But Billy felt miserable. Why couldn't he slow down and preach like a real preacher?

When they returned to school, Dean Minder asked Billy to be the youth director at the Tampa Gospel Tabernacle.

"Me?" asked Billy, still bothered by his experience in Bostwick.

"Our youth group is small and discouraged, and

"ME?"

you're just the man to pep them up."

Billy threw himself into the new job with his usual energy. The teens in Tampa were seeking God. They responded to Billy's loud, arm-waving prayers. The group grew larger. Billy was thrilled that he could lead. Maybe he was cut out to serve God after all.

Not all his experiences in Florida were warm glowing ones. Once in Tampa, Billy saw a man hit by a car. The man writhed and screamed that he was lost, slipping to hell. What could be more frightening than eternity in hell? Any time Billy weakened in his efforts, he would think of that man lying on the brink of eternal torture. Eternal hell.

Night after night, Billy lay awake in his dorm room, tormented by his doubts. Was he really meant to preach? Sometimes he got up to wander the grounds, even roaming the spongy fairways of the golf course. He brooded on and on, unable to sleep,

WAS HE REALLY MEANT TO PREACH?

wandering in lonely misery.

Help me, God, he prayed.

On one cool night in the spring of 1938, Billy sat down on the eighteenth green, facing the dark sloping fairway. Suddenly the doubt lifted. Flickering through his mind were images of rallies, throngs of folks spread before a platform higher than a throne. He knew in his heart that somehow he was going to be a small part of that vision.

Billy got on his knees. "The first commandment is to love the Lord my God with all my heart and with all my soul and with all my mind. I surrender, Lord! If You want me to spread the gospel by preaching, I will!"

Billy threw himself into his relationship with Christ. He prayed for hours on end. He read the Bible as he never had before. He was appointed assistant pastor of the Tampa Gospel Tabernacle.

That was not enough. Billy became the preacher

BILLY GOT ON HIS KNEES

to a trailer park. He preached to Cuban-Americans through an interpreter. He preached on the student radio station. He stalked the streets of Tampa. No sinner was safe. Once when Billy preached on a sidewalk in downtown Tampa, a man whacked him sprawling into the street.

"It is an honor to suffer for Christ," said Billy, surveying the dirt on his suit like it was gold. He meant it. He really felt the Holy Spirit inside him.

But Billy still had doubts. He bounced around the pulpit, flailed the air with his arms like a man swatting flies, and boomed his raw North Carolina twang off the ceilings. He jabbed his finger. His message was plain vanilla: You are a sinner. Christ died to pay for your sins. But you must accept Christ to be saved.

Does God want me to preach this way? he asked himself. No one else preached so fast and furiously. Results are what count, aren't they? Can I, or can I

"IT IS AN HONOR TO SUFFER FOR CHRIST."

not, bring sinners to accept Christ and His salvation? Billy had never called people to the altar after his sermon to accept Christ. The regular pastor did that.

There was only one way for Billy to get the answer. I've got to test myself, he resolved.

And he faced the test with fear and trembling.

I'VE GOT TO TEST MYSELF, HE RESOLVED.

AS HE PREACHED, HE FELT THE HOLY SPIRIT HELPING HIM.

6

When the night for his first altar call came, Billy gnawed his fingernails, sick with worry. He had prayed all afternoon for God's help. "I'll have to quit preaching if I fail," he glumly reminded himself. "If I can't bring folks to the altar to accept Christ, I'm just making a lot of noise."

One hundred people were in the congregation that night to listen to Billy preach. Heart thumping, he began. As he preached, he felt the Holy Spirit helping him. Arms flailing and words exploding like gunfire, he delivered the gospel. But at the end of his sermon, his heart was in his mouth.

"Now, friends, if you want your life to change tonight," he said, "come forward now and accept Christ as your Savior." His mouth was dry as desert sand. Had his loud preaching turned people away from Christ?

Hands clasped, eyes down, Billy waited in sweaty humility. Surely at least one person would come. Oh please, God, just one. All he wanted was one. If only he could lead one sinner to Jesus. Billy waited. What if no one came?

Slowly, a man stood up. Was the man going to come to the altar or was he simply leaving the church? The man hesitated. Sin was so hard to acknowledge publicly. The man slowly turned to the altar. Yes! He was coming forward. Oh, praise the Lord!

Another person stood up. Could it be that she was coming to Christ, too? Or was she leaving? She came forward. Oh, yes. Praise the Lord.

Then another. And another.

Soon, people were rising so fast Billy could no longer count. He wanted to weep. He wasn't worthy

PEOPLE WERE RISING SO FAST
BILLY COULD NO LONGER COUNT.

of this. Oh, rebuke me, God, he prayed. This was not my sermon. It was not my personal charm. God forgive me for even thinking that. The sinners are coming to Christ because the Holy Spirit was working through me.

"Thirty-two came to the altar," said one member of the church later. "In all my years, I never saw so many come to the altar in one meeting. You have something special, Billy Graham."

By early 1940, Billy was close to graduating from the institute. What was he going to do then? In the meantime he was still a student, doing all the chores students did. One day he was caddying for two golfers named Elmer Edman and Paul Fisher.

Paul Fisher said, "We're from Wheaton, Illinois."

Billy gushed, "Where Wheaton College is located? What a coincidence. My mother always dreamed of me going there, but we couldn't afford it."

"YOU HAVE SOMETHING SPECIAL, BILLY GRAHAM."

Fisher set his jaw. "I'll pay your room and board for one year."

Elmer Edman said, "And I'll pay your tuition for a year. After that, I expect you can get a scholarship. The truth is, we want Wheaton College to graduate Billy Graham."

"So we can claim you," said Fisher.

"If that doesn't beat all. Me?" said Billy. "Mother will be so happy."

So Billy went to Wheaton College in 1940. But he eyed Europe nervously. The continent was in the murderous grip of the Germans, corrupted by Adolph Hitler and his evil Nazi party. Would America have to fight the Germans?

Billy arrived at Wheaton College nearly twenty-two years old and an ordained minister, yet a mere freshman. He was a curiosity at first, the gangly smiley southerner in his summery suits and bright ties. But all he had to do was lead one prayer in a

BILLY WENT TO WHEATON COLLEGE IN 1940.

student meeting and those present never looked at him the same way again.

Billy met Ruth Bell. She was the daughter of missionaries in China. Dark-haired, she had sharp features and wide thin lips, but her face was softened by amber eyes, creamy complexion, and complete innocence. Most girls gawked at Billy, but not Ruth. She hardly looked at him.

Billy immediately fell in love with her. He thought about her all the time. So he nervously invited her to a performance of Messiah. It seemed an eternity before she accepted!

Ruth was a perfect spiritual mate for Billy. The problem was that Ruth wanted to be a missionary. The more Billy thought about Ruth Bell, the more troubled he became. How could her goals ever be reconciled with his own goals? Could he rob this godly woman of her destiny? He backed off. Let God decide.

BILLY MET RUTH BELL.

Many weeks later, Billy received a letter from Ruth: an invitation to a party. So it is God's will, he told himself.

Over the months, they saw each other often. Ruth was saintly. Her worn Bible had notes penciled in all the margins. She loved animals like Billy did. Animals were God's creatures. Ruth couldn't find a dead bird without burying it. To think of that precious creature lying out in the open made her sick.

Billy had never met anyone as fascinating as Ruth. She added a new dimension to his life. Longing for her gnawed at him constantly. Finally he decided he would ask Ruth to marry him and let God sort their careers out. Let God's will be done.

Billy asked Ruth to marry him. Ruth accepted and a little while later visited the Graham family in Charlotte, wearing her engagement ring. Billy's father was pleased with Billy's choices for both a wife and a calling. He said, "Some folks are saying the night

BILLY ASKED RUTH TO MARRY HIM.

Mordecai Ham snatched up Billy here for Christ was the very same night Billy Sunday died. . ."

Billy was shocked. "Daddy, you never told me that before."

"I'm not sure it's true. Anyway, that's what some folks are saying."

"The great Billy Sunday. Imagine," mumbled Billy.

On December 7, 1941, the calm on the campus at Wheaton College exploded. Japanese planes had bombed the American naval base at Pearl Harbor in the Pacific Ocean. The next day, America declared war on Japan, and three days later, America declared war on Germany. World War II had begun for America!

Billy wanted to enlist as a soldier. Professors talked him out of it. Could he kill another man? If he couldn't, he was only endangering his fellow soldiers. So Billy tried to enlist as a chaplain, a man of

JAPANESE PLANES HAD BOMBED PEARL HARBOR.

God. The army told him he not only had to finish his college work first, but he also needed one year as a full pastor to qualify as a chaplain.

In 1943 Billy graduated from Wheaton College. He was offered a pastorship in nearby Western Springs, Illinois. The small basement church of thirty-five members was barely surviving, but Billy was undaunted. He could hardly wait to get started as a real pastor.

Yet he had another great event in his life to take care of first. After three years of courtship, Billy married Ruth at Montreat, North Carolina, where Ruth's parents lived.

When the Billy Grahams returned to Illinois, Billy began pastoring at Western Springs. The members were stunned by his sin-prodding, machine-gun delivery. But more and more people joined the church. And most important, Billy persuaded them to come to the altar to accept Christ.

BILLY MARRIED RUTH AT MONTREAT, NORTH CAROLINA.

"You really do have the power of the Holy Spirit," said Ruth in awe.

Billy was awed too, when he had time to stop and reflect. But he stayed very busy. It seemed almost overnight that he started a prayer group of prominent businessmen. He welcomed their donations to his church because the money could do so much toward spreading the gospel.

Opportunities seemed to seek Billy out. They found him because he was everywhere, opening doors. One day he was approached with an offer from Torrey Johnson, another pastor. Billy rushed home to Ruth with news of Pastor Johnson's offer. This opportunity seemed a hundred times greater than anything before.

"YOU REALLY DO HAVE THE POWER OF THE HOLY SPIRIT."

"HE OFFERED ME HIS RADIO PROGRAM."

7

"Torrey Johnson started too many activities," Billy explained to Ruth. "He has to cut back. He offered me his radio program. It's broadcast by WCFL —50,000 watts. My parents and your parents will hear me way down in North Carolina, especially since we broadcast late at night."

By the beginning of 1944 Billy was welcoming radio listeners to Songs in the Night from "the friendly church in the pleasant community of Western Springs." Following a hymn sung by Bev Shea, Billy burst in over a background of bad news with a sermon on the urgent need for Christ.

Billy had smoothed his twang into a honeyed southern accent. The radio program proved that Billy's power to persuade people wasn't from his blue eyes or his lion's mane of golden hair. He was very popular. Donations from listeners poured in to the church.

Torrey Johnson next asked Billy to help him with revival meetings. Billy was eager to help. First the revivals were for soldiers in the Chicago area. Then they expanded to all the young people around Chicago. Finally the meetings were for young people nationwide.

Suddenly Billy was preaching to crowds of ten thousand! It happened so fast that he never had a chance to be overwhelmed by what he was doing. Torrey Johnson had him traveling all over America, making arrangements for future rallies of Youth for Christ.

By early 1945, Billy was so busy with Torrey Johnson's rallies that he could no longer do his radio program or even pastor his church. Ruth urged him to choose. Was Billy going to be a traveling

SUDDENLY BILLY WAS PREACHING
TO CROWDS OF TEN THOUSAND!

evangelist or a pastor of a church? She thought it was impossible to be both. Billy chose evangelism. Ruth was happy with his choice.

Preaching and planning rallies for teens meant Billy had to travel constantly. Ruth missed him but joked she would rather have a little of Billy than a lot of anybody else. She left Illinois to live with her parents in Montreat, North Carolina.

Billy understood. People serving Christ had to make sacrifices. Besides, America was at war, and President Franklin Roosevelt had died suddenly. Billy not only mourned the dead president but prayed for his successor, Harry Truman.

One month later the Germans surrendered. By September the Japanese had surrendered, and World War II was over. Over ten million young Americans returned from the war to resume their lives.

Ruth gave birth to their daughter Virginia on September 21. Ruth nicknamed her "GiGi," Chinese

RUTH WAS HAPPY WITH HIS CHOICE.

for sister.

The Youth for Christ movement had become such a national sensation that President Truman praised it. Time magazine ran a story on it. The newspaper empire of William Randolph Hearst assigned one reporter full-time to cover the movement.

The Youth for Christ organization got local clergy to counsel those who came to Christ. That made a revival much more effective but also much more difficult to plan. Advance planning became a very big job—and it was Billy's.

Torrey Johnson decided it was time Youth for Christ became international. The team that left for England included Torrey Johnson and Billy.

The English were shocked by Billy. They had no pastors who preached in bright red bow ties and pink suits. Their pastors did not stalk the platform, bending down, bolting upright, flailing their arms. They had no pastors who spoke at the rate of 240 words

THE ENGLISH WERE SHOCKED BY BILLY.

per minute and never used an adjective or adverb.

Billy's simple message of sin and salvation spattered the audience like machine gun fire. There was no escape. Most stunning of all to the English was the stream of sinners coming to the altar to accept Christ after Billy called them.

Back in America, anticipation of a series of revival meetings for Youth for Christ in Charlotte created one of Billy's black moments of doubt. What if he failed in his own backyard?

"We've got to go all out for Charlotte," he said nervously to Ruth.

Billy chewed his nails. He spurred an advance campaign that went far beyond the usual billboards, bumper stickers, radio commercials, and placards in buses and windows. Billy had airplanes zooming over Charlotte, trailing banners, and dropping leaflets. He gave daily press releases to thirty-one local newspapers. He hired variety acts.

"WE'VE GOT TO GO ALL OUT FOR CHARLOTTE."

Billy hired Cliff Barrows, Bev Shea, and his old buddy Grady Wilson. Grady was married now, with his own ministry in South Carolina. He was still just as quick-witted and sharp-tongued as ever. He knew how to keep Billy's feet on the ground. Billy loved Grady.

Yet Billy still had doubts. "Lord, don't let me fail in my own backyard."

Billy's revival meetings at Charlotte drew forty-two thousand people. As usual, if people could be gathered, Billy could persuade many of them to come to Christ.

The team of Billy, Cliff Barrows, Bev Shea, and Grady Wilson worked well together. Grady was Billy's jack of all trades. He could organize prayer groups, preach if Billy got sick, tell funny stories, or cook breakfast. Burly song-leader Cliff, swinging his trombone, bounced through the singing like a cheerleader. Dignified Bev preceded Billy's sermon

"LORD, DON'T LET ME FAIL IN MY OWN BACKYARD."

with a hymn to set a serious tone.

So Billy's black moment had become one of his greatest leaps forward. He felt so good about his team that he wanted to go out on his own to evangelize.

In Montreat, Billy bought a house across the street from Ruth's parents. In May 1948 another daughter was born: Anne.

Billy drew away from the Youth for Christ organization more and more. He wanted to offer salvation to people of all ages. Finally he went on his own.

In 1949 Billy had his biggest test yet. For three weeks his organization hoped to pack six thousand people, six nights a week and twice on Sunday, into Billy's Canvas Cathedral—a huge, three-spired circus tent in downtown Los Angeles.

The campaign had the support of local churches as well as the mayor and local celebrities like Stuart Hamblen, a singing Texan with a daily radio program. Most important to Billy's sense that all would go

BILLY'S CANVAS CATHEDRAL.

well was the presence of his team: Grady Wilson, Cliff Barrows, and Bev Shea.

Since they now embraced a wider audience than just teens, Billy toned down the service so that it was more a church service and less of a colorful show. His gaudy clothing was gone. He usually wore dark suits.

Clutching his black Bible, Billy would borrow an old-time evangelist's phrase and bellow, "The Bible says," and go on to quote Scripture. Then he would begin to condemn those who disobeyed God's Word and explain the dreaded consequences: everlasting hell.

Billy wore a microphone on the lapel of his coat so he could be heard in the farthest corners of the tent. He still stalked the platform, cracking out words in a honeyed southern accent like pops of lightning. He locked his eyes on several hundred sinners at once.

HE STALKED THE PLATFORM.

When he had thousands of them squirming, it was time for a change of pace. He would soften his tone for a while. Billy hammered through the list of sins: love of material things, alcoholism, adultery, suicide, stealing, cheating, greed.

No one was safe. The radio star Stuart Hamblen, who had a reputation for wild living, quickly found that out. Billy pistoled his finger in Hamblen's direction and snapped, "There's a man in here leading a double life!" The next night he leveled his finger at Hamblen again: "There's a phony in here tonight!" After that night Hamblen refused to attend.

The local committee asked Billy if he wanted to extend the revival beyond three weeks. Billy had never extended a revival before, no matter how successful, because he always had others planned. But this time was different.

"I'll ask for a sign from God," Billy said nervously, "like Gideon did in the book of Judges when

"I'LL ASK FOR A SIGN FROM GOD."

he put out a fleece. Gideon had to know if God wanted him to do a certain thing, so one night he put a sheepskin outside on the ground. If in the morning the fleece was covered with dew, yet the ground around it was completely dry, that would be a sign from God to go ahead. And God gave Gideon the sign to go ahead: the fleece was wet."

"But what will be your sign, Billy?" asked one of the team.

"I don't know," he admitted nervously.

"WHAT WILL BE YOUR SIGN, BILLY?"

BILLY GOT A CALL FROM STUART HAMBLEN.

8

Billy got a phone call from Stuart Hamblen in the middle of the night. He wanted to repent his sins and accept Christ. Hamblen's change of heart was miraculous, surely a sign from God to continue the revival in Los Angeles.

"Please, Lord, help Stuart convert from sinner to Your faithful servant," prayed Billy.

On his radio program, Hamblen announced he had repented, promising to give up alcohol, cigarettes, even all his racehorses—except El Lobo, who was like a family pet. After several days, Stuart's decision to become a servant of Christ seemed real.

Not long after that success, Louis Zamperini came to the altar. Zamperini had been a world-class distance runner and a hero in World War II, but finally his great courage failed him. Until Billy brought him to Christ, he tried to find courage in a whiskey bottle.

Success snowballed. Another man came to the altar. He was a crook for a notorious Los Angeles gangster. Curious Hollywood celebrities began to attend the revivals to see who was salvaging all these fallen men.

Suddenly the revival was being touted in the Los Angeles newspapers of William Randolph Hearst, with full-page stories and photos of Billy preaching to the crowd like John the Baptist. A few days later reporters from the national magazines Life, Newsweek, and Time showed up.

"That's wonderful," gushed Billy.

But Billy was exhausted. Fatigue is a tool of the devil, he told himself. "The more tired I become physically, the stronger I must become spiritually," he declared, echoing the apostle Paul.

Finally, on November 20, the tent meetings came

THE REVIVAL TOUTED IN THE LOS ANGELES NEWSPAPER.

to an end. For that last meeting, the crowd overflowed the Canvas Cathedral into the street, blocking traffic. In eight weeks in Los Angeles, Billy had drawn 350,000 listeners!

"It will be kind of nice to get away from all the hubbub for a while," said Billy as he boarded the train to go east the next day.

But the train was no refuge. Billy was amazed to discover that everyone seemed to know him. At Kansas City, reporters rushed inside the train, rudely asking questions and taking photographs. He wanted to tell them to back off, but wouldn't he be betraying his friends? Wasn't this the publicity the revival movement needed?

Billy followed Los Angeles with revivals in Boston and South Carolina. They were successful, too. At the University of South Carolina, Billy filled the football stadium with forty thousand people hungry for Christ. Ten thousand had to be turned

THE TRAIN WAS NO REFUGE.

away. It was the first time he called his revival a crusade.

Word of his successful crusades spread like wildfire to the highest circles of the country. Billy was invited to pray before the United States Congress in Washington, D.C.

Billy was increasingly nervous about success. It was all so much, so fast. Would he falter? He had to remind himself that Billy Graham wasn't going to succeed or falter. His success was God's success. But the reporters kept turning it into Billy Graham's success. And he had to keep repeating, "No, no, this is God's glory."

Billy was determined not to take credit for his success. He believed that if he did, his power would end as suddenly as it had for Moses when he struck the rock at Kadesh.

In Billy's experience, people suffered from four miseries: emptiness, loneliness, guilt, and fear of

HIS SUCCESS WAS GOD'S SUCCESS.

death. Unless he was aiming at a specific audience like teenagers and how they could enlist Christ to fight sexual temptation, he would preach on one of those main four human miseries. Of course, the answer to these miseries was Christ.

During the call to the altar, Billy would plant his chin in his right hand, reminding himself that people were responding to the Holy Spirit, not to Billy Graham. And yet when people came forward, Billy tried to look every one of them in the eye. Who could know if that extra encouragement might make their conversion just a little stronger? They were babes in Christ. They had to be encouraged in every way.

He said the "sinner's prayer" with them: Oh God, I am a sinner. I'm sorry for my sins. I'm willing to turn from my sins. I receive Christ as my Savior. I confess Him as my Lord. From this moment on I want to follow Him and serve Him in the fellowship of the church. In Christ's name, Amen.

THEY HAD TO BE ENCOURAGED IN EVERY WAY.

Then volunteers from local churches counseled the new believers in Christ on what to do next.

After one crusade, Billy received an invitation. He was stunned. He asked Grady, "What do we have scheduled for July 14, 1950?"

"Let me see."

"Never mind. Cancel it. We've been invited to the White House."

Grady was excited. "The White House? To meet President Truman? How should we dress?"

"What do you mean?" asked Billy. "Wear a dark suit and black shoes."

"But Truman is a very casual guy. Haven't you seen pictures of him in Florida at Key West in his spiffy white buck shoes and colorful Hawaiian shirts?"

"We can't wear Hawaiian shirts to the White House," argued Billy.

"What about white bucks?"

"WE'VE BEEN INVITED TO THE WHITE HOUSE."

"That would definitely break the ice," enthused Billy. "We could wear light summer suits, hand-painted ties, and white buck shoes. We'll let the president know we're down-to-earth folks—just like he is."

And that's how Billy, Cliff Barrows, and Grady Wilson dressed for the White House. The president greeted them, standing ramrod straight in a dark suit. After they chatted a few minutes, Billy ended the meeting with a prayer. Reporters flocked around Billy as he left the White House. He was very pleased with his meeting. He told them what had been said.

The next day one of the team told Billy, "The newspaper says we really goofed. We shouldn't have talked about what was said in the meeting. The president is real mad about it."

"Oh Lord, how puffed up we were," said Billy, remembering.

"My son, despise not the chastening of the Lord;

THE PRESIDENT GREETED THEM.

neither be weary of his correction," quoted Ruth. "Isn't that one of your favorite verses?" she added not so innocently.

"Proverbs 3:11," confirmed Billy. "Amen. God yanked us up short and booted us right in the seat of our pants!"

Billy moved on to his Portland crusade. It was difficult for him to walk about freely. People swarmed all around him as if he were a celebrity. He spent more and more time in his hotel room when he wasn't preaching. He would remain in his room, dressed very casually, wearing a green baseball cap to keep his unruly hair matted down, until he finally left to preach in the afternoon or evening.

Things were happening at a feverish pace. On November 5, 1950, Billy launched his new weekly radio program across the entire nation. The program opened with the stirring "Battle Hymn of the Republic," followed by Cliff Barrows who finished his

"GOD BOOTED US RIGHT IN THE SEAT OF OUR PANTS!"

introduction with: "This is the 'Hour of Decision'!"

Then Grady Wilson would read a passage from the Bible, and Bev Shea would sing a hymn. Next Billy would relate current news items to the Bible. Then relentlessly, never faltering once for a word, he warned his listeners of impending hell without Christ.

At his crusade in Atlanta, Billy met the widow of the great evangelist Billy Sunday. Ma Sunday, as she was called, had some bitter advice.

"Boys," she said, "I know you have to travel night and day to spread the gospel. It's the Great Commission in the last chapter of the book of Matthew. But don't let your wives neglect your kids. I thought I had to travel all over the country with Billy Sunday. We trashed the lives of our own kids." Tears streamed down her face.

Billy had felt very guilty about leaving Ruth behind in North Carolina with GiGi and Anne. Because

"THIS IS THE HOUR OF DECISION!"

of Ma Sunday's torment, he would never feel guilty again. But he would miss Ruth and his children very much when he was gone.

Billy formed a corporation because so much money was pouring in. That way he could account for every penny that was donated. It was very important that people know he wasn't getting rich from their donations. His organization was called the Billy Graham Evangelical Association, or just BGEA.

With weekly radio programs and never-ending city-wide crusades, the demands on Billy's organization were great. The headquarters of BGEA in Minneapolis, Minnesota, added people to write scripts and take care of a thousand details. And if 1950 wasn't busy enough, Ruth gave birth to their third daughter on December 19. The infant Ruth was nicknamed "Bunny."

In 1950 Billy had begun a film company too, one that would later be called World Wide Pictures.

TEARS STREAMED DOWN HER FACE.

And since more and more Americans owned television sets, he felt the need to start a weekly television show called "Hour of Decision."

"I learned long ago to open as many doors as possible," he reminded critics. He wasn't going to neglect any promising approach to spreading the gospel.

Billy's city-wide crusades were changing for the better. He had stopped asking for offerings. His radio and television shows caused money to pour in to BGEA in Minneapolis, where every penny was carefully accounted for.

One iron-clad requirement for a city-wide crusade was that a majority of the local churches had to invite his crusade. That way Billy knew the city really wanted it and would furnish plenty of volunteers to counsel all those who came to the altar to accept Christ.

But another urgent need was gnawing at him.

HE FELT THE NEED TO START A WEEKLY TELEVISION SHOW.

SEPARATING THE RACES WAS NOT IN CHRIST'S TEACHINGS.

9

Billy always called people to the altar together, declaring pointedly, "The ground is level at the foot of the cross. I want all white folks, all black folks to come forward together ."

In 1951 in many parts of America, white people still kept the races separate in schools and on buses and in other ways. Billy knew separating the races was not in Christ's teachings. But he thought white folks had to be won over gradually to allow integration.

Billy wasn't a hypocrite. It was the same way he handled prejudice against himself. He never tore into someone because they criticized him or let him down. He approached them with love and friendly persuasion. But Billy knew blacks had to have equal justice and equal opportunities.

In 1952 Billy held a crusade in Washington, D.C. The Speaker of the House of Representatives, Sam Rayburn, praised him. "This country needs a revival, and I believe Billy Graham is bringing it to us."

With one nod from the powerful Speaker Rayburn, Billy gained what had seemed impossible: he got to hold his final rally on the steps of the Capitol! Billy had drawn over 300,000 people in five weeks. He made many friends among powerful politicians in both political parties. Among them were Lyndon Johnson and Richard Nixon.

Billy kept expanding his organization during 1952. In addition to his radio and television shows, he started a weekly newspaper column called "My Answer," in which he answered people's problems with Scripture. His family kept growing, too. Franklin was born July 14. The Grahams had four children. Ruth rarely traveled with Billy. One of the few times

HE STARTED A WEEKLY NEWSPAPER COLUMN.

she did was on a trip to Korea.

America was involved in a war, trying to protect South Korea against the communists of North Korea and China. Billy went to South Korea in late 1952. In a hospital, one severely wounded soldier, suspended face down in a contraption, begged to see Billy. So Billy crawled underneath to lie on the floor and pray with the soldier. Billy had seen some of the horror and heartbreak the soldiers knew. He prayed harder than ever for the war to end.

On the way back to America he told Ruth, "I feel like I went to Korea a boy and I'm coming back a man."

The Korean experience reminded Billy of another problem. Black soldiers were dying right beside white soldiers. When was the separation of races in some parts of America going to stop?

In March 1953 at his Chattanooga crusade, Billy declared, "Jesus Christ belongs neither to the black

BILLY CRAWLED UNDERNEATH TO PRAY WITH THE SOLDIER.

nor the white races. There are no color lines with Christ, as he repeatedly said that God looks upon the heart." Billy had to keep crusading to change the hearts of some prejudiced white people.

Even though Billy had not been appreciated by Harry Truman, he did get off on the right foot with the man who'd just been elected the new president. Dwight Eisenhower was a World War II hero known to everyone as "Ike."

Billy gave Ike a red Bible. Ike seemed to really like Billy. He had asked Billy for advice on the speech he made after the ceremony in which he was sworn in as the new president.

In July 1953, the fighting in Korea stopped. Billy couldn't imagine a greater evil than godless communism. He thanked God that the fighting in Korea was over.

Next, he sat down with Ruth to write a book. Friends offered helpful criticism, and Billy and Ruth

IKE SEEMED TO REALLY LIKE BILLY.

wrote the book again. Billy was very proud of the book. Surely this was God's doing.

He mailed it to a publisher in New York. The Doubleday Company published the book late in 1953. They named the book *Peace with God*.

"Can't we relax for a while?" asked Ruth.

"We have a crusade in England." Billy's schedule seemed endless.

He drew such large crowds in England that his hosts set up a network of sites, with Billy's sermon relayed to each site by telephone. Each sermon was heard at over 400 churches and rented halls in 175 cities in Great Britain and Ireland. At each site, the local clergy talked to the audience before the sermon and counseled them afterward, just as they did in the arena where Billy preached.

At a London school, a student suddenly disrupted Billy's sermon by leaping about and scratching like an ape.

THEY NAMED THE BOOK PEACE WITH GOD.

"He reminds me of my ancestors," quipped Billy.

The students roared with laughter, sure the American evangelist had been caught admitting evolution was true, that people were descended from apes.

Billy added, "Of course, all my ancestors came from Great Britain."

On the last day of the crusade, Billy spoke to 120,000 people in Wembley Stadium. The day was such a success that the very formal and proper Archbishop of Canterbury murmured, "I don't think we'll ever see a sight like this again until we get to heaven."

Grady Wilson gave the archbishop a bear hug and hooted, "That's right, Brother Archbishop! That's right!"

At noon on May 24, 1954, Billy found himself inside Number Ten Downing Street talking to none other than the British Prime Minister: the legendary Winston Churchill.

THE LEGENDARY WINSTON CHURCHILL.

"Is there any hope for this world?" Churchill asked suddenly.

Billy was shocked. Was this the giant whose speeches gave the British people hope against the Nazi war machine in World War II? Or was he testing Billy?

Billy reached in his coat pocket and pulled out his New Testament. "Mr. Prime Minister, this fills me with hope!" And Billy punched out the message of Christ in his simple, direct way. Miraculously, Churchill allowed Billy to talk on and on. Before they parted, Billy assured him in prayer, "God is the hope for the world you despair for."

Billy didn't tell reporters what he had talked about with Prime Minister Churchill. He only said that he felt like he had talked to "Mr. History."

In London Billy had preached to two million people, either in person or by telephone relay.

In 1955 Billy was once again across the Atlantic

"IS THERE ANY HOPE FOR THIS WORLD?"

Ocean, this time for his All-Scotland Crusade. The response night after night was so enthusiastic that the organizers telephoned broadcasts of the crusade into the rest of Great Britain and Ireland.

"Are you ready for the finale?" asked Grady, trying to act casual.

"If the Holy Spirit is," answered Billy nervously.

The meetings were going to end with the Good Friday meeting which BBC Television was televising to all of Britain. Only Queen Elizabeth's coronation had been watched by so many British people.

The day after Good Friday, people all over Britain were talking about Billy's sermon. Reviews were glowing. Later, he was allowed to preach privately to young Queen Elizabeth and her court at Windsor Castle.

President Eisenhower said that Billy Graham understood that "any advance in the world has got to be accompanied by a clear realization that man is,

HE PREACHED PRIVATELY TO YOUNG QUEEN ELIZABETH.

after all, a spiritual being ."

In North Carolina Ruth and the children were in a new home: Little Piney Cove, located on property Billy and Ruth had bought several years earlier. Ruth drove Billy in a Jeep along a winding road to their new home.

"Are you sure you want to be way up here on the mountain?" asked Billy.

"Ever since the trip to England in 1954, the tourists haven't left us alone. When I caught Bunny opening her small red purse to collect money from tourists in return for posing for pictures, I knew then and there we had to move!"

Now the Grahams had privacy in a large, U-shaped house constructed of logs Ruth scrounged from old cabins. Below yawned a pine-covered valley. Above, clinging to the mountainside, thorny black-berry bushes fringed a forest of pine, aspen, and maple trees.

"ARE YOU SURE YOU WANT TO BE
WAY UP HERE ON THE MOUNTAIN?"

It rained often at Little Piney Cove. Soft rain seemed wonderful to Ruth; it depressed Billy. Because he fretted and gnawed his fingernails so much, the children dubbed him "Puddleglum," a lovable but pessimistic character in *The Silver Chair* by C. S. Lewis.

"Is the King dead? Has the enemy landed in Narnia?" giggled the children. GiGi was almost eleven, Anne eight, Bunny five, and Franklin three. They read all the Narnia books by C. S. Lewis.

In 1956 Billy helped Ruth's father Nelson Bell launch a new magazine. Christianity Today was one more improvement in the evangelical machine Billy had built. He spread the gospel through crusades, movies, radio, television, a newspaper column, and a book. People had even named Billy's movement the "New Evangelicalism."

Billy said, "I believe that every word of the Bible is true and inspired by God. I believe God has

IT RAINED OFTEN AT LITTLE PINEY COVE.

existed forever as the Father, the Son, and the Holy Spirit. I believe Christ, born of a virgin, died for our sins, rose again, and will come again. I believe all people are sinners. I believe sinners can be saved only through accepting Christ as their Savior. These are beliefs held by all evangelicals. But if folks want to label me a New Evangelical, that's fine with me."

Billy never liked to quarrel.

"SINNERS CAN BE SAVED ONLY THROUGH ACCEPTING CHRIST."

THE REVEREND MARTIN LUTHER KING JR.

10

In May 1957 Billy crusaded in New York. The results were staggering. Night after night in Madison Square Garden, Billy preached to nearly twenty thousand people.

Billy invited the Reverend Martin Luther King Jr., the black civil rights leader, to open one service in prayer. Billy wanted folks to see that whites and blacks work together for God. His comments in magazine interviews were more blunt: hating anyone because of the color of his skin is a sin.

Nearing the end of sixteen weeks in New York, Billy had lost thirty pounds. "But I can do all things through Christ which strengtheneth me," he said, quoting Philippians 4:13, one of his favorite verses. And he went on to draw 100,000 people into Yankee Stadium.

The last day of the New York crusade, Billy drew 200,000 people into Times Square. A grand total of 2.3 million people had attended the crusade.

"To God be all the glory," Billy told everyone. "This is His doing, and let no one fail to give Him the credit."

Then a confrontation held the attention of all America. The Arkansas governor was defying the Supreme Court's 1954 ruling that all public schools had to integrate. The Court had decided that officials couldn't keep black and white children in separate schools. The governor of Arkansas refused to allow black students to enter Central High School in Little Rock.

Billy got a phone call from the White House. Ike had been asking him for advice on racial matters. What did Billy think about Ike sending soldiers to Little Rock to force integration?

"Do it, Mr. President," advised Billy.

That afternoon, hard-nosed paratroopers of the

"DO IT, MR. PRESIDENT."

101st Airborne Division entered Little Rock. Central High School was integrated.

A second son, Nelson, was born January 12, 1958, and immediately dubbed "Ned." Billy continued to crusade.

That fall, white racists bombed a high school in Clinton, Tennessee. The school had just been integrated. Billy stepped forward to declare, "Every Christian should take his stand against these outrages."

In December Billy spoke in Clinton to an audience of five thousand people to raise money for a new school, calling for "forgiveness, cool heads, and warm hearts."

One day in January 1959 when Billy was playing golf, he kept missing the ball. "The ground has ridges in it," he explained to Grady.

Grady chuckled. "Lord have mercy. That's a new excuse, buddy."

Suddenly pain stabbed Billy's left eye.

"LORD HAVE MERCY. THAT'S A NEW EXCUSE BUDDY."

At a clinic, doctors found that forty-year-old Billy had an eye disease. He was ordered to rest. But he could never be idle. He and Grady Wilson, along with their wives, studied the Bible very hard as Billy rested.

"This is surely God's way of making me recharge my spiritual batteries," said Billy.

He established a routine for Bible reading that he hoped would stay with him forever. Every day he read five Psalms and a chapter of Proverbs so that he would read through both books every month. Proverbs instructed him on how to deal with other people. Psalms inspired him to talk to God. In addition Billy read enough of the rest of Scripture each day to get completely through the Bible once each year.

In 1959 Billy held very successful crusades in Australia and New Zealand. Back in America Billy held two rallies in Little Rock. Racist groups mounted hate campaigns against him. But Billy, practicing the

VERY DAY HE READ FIVE PSALMS AND A CHAPTER OF PROVERBS.

gospel of love, talked to everyone, trying to heal Little Rock of its bitterness. At the revivals, local pastors were stunned to see known white racists coming to the altar to repent of their sins and accept Christ. Little Rock was recovering.

In January 1960 Billy started to crusade through Africa. When he found out that blacks could not attend his rallies in the country of South Africa, he refused to go there.

At Kaduna, Nigeria, Billy was invited to visit a leper colony. He steeled himself against the sight of faces eaten away by the terrible disease. He preached to the residents, assuring them that God loved them and that a new spiritual body awaited them in heaven.

As he was about to leave, a small, maimed woman shuffled toward him, extending an envelope with fingerless hands. It was a love offering from the people with leprosy for Billy's ministry.

"Boys," he told Grady and Cliff, "that's what the

IT WAS A LOVE OFFERING FROM THE PEOPLE WITH LEPROSY.

ministry is all about." Tears scalded his cheeks. This woman was like the widow in Luke 21, who gave two tiny copper coins—everything she had.

In America during the fall of 1961, Billy's crusade in Philadelphia included seven students from a seminary, a school for ministers. Why not let seminary students learn how to evangelize from the most effective evangelist in the world? After Philadelphia the number of students, or interns, grew with every crusade.

Billy had always resisted the idea of his own school. "Maybe this is the form God wants my school to take: on-the-job training at the Billy Graham School of Evangelism."

In 1962 Billy was saddened by his seventy-four-year-old father's death. Billy didn't have to worry about his mother's financial security. Frank had quietly amassed a fortune. Not only had the dairy been profitable, but Frank's land had sprouted office buildings as the city of Charlotte grew and grew.

THIS WOMAN WAS LIKE THE WIDOW IN LUKE 21.

The following May, Billy's daughter GiGi married Stephan Tchividjian. Pleased, Billy told Ruth, "Many times I have prayed for such husbands for our daughters."

But 1963 was to be a year of turmoil. Blacks were going to jail, rallying in protest marches, and integrating formerly all-white schools all over America. Billy supported their efforts. Some criticized him for wanting to go too slow; some criticized him for wanting to go too fast.

But the most shocking event of 1963 took place in November as Billy was playing golf near Montreat.

"Somebody shot at the president in a motorcade in Dallas!" yelled someone.

"Surely not!" said Billy.

But President John Kennedy had been shot and killed. Billy was sick. What a tragedy! Lyndon Johnson was sworn in as the new president. Billy offered his services to Johnson. Within one month, he was invited to the White House for a fifteen-minute meeting.

PRESIDENT JOHN KENNEDY HAD BEEN SHOT AND KILLED.

Johnson's creased face showed terrible strain, and Billy brought him the peace of God. Fifteen minutes became five hours. They swam in the White House pool. Johnson relaxed even more under Grady Wilson's endless barrage of jokes.

Billy cemented the friendship by telling reporters, "Lyndon Johnson is the most qualified man ever to take on the presidency."

In 1964 Lyndon Johnson was reelected president. He asked Billy to visit Selma, Alabama, where civil rights workers had been murdered. Billy also held a large integrated rally in Birmingham, where a black church had been bombed. Thirty-five thousand people, half black and half white, attended.

Billy supported Lyndon Johnson's new Great Society programs, aimed at helping poor people of all races. But Billy was worried about something else. American soldiers were being sent to the far-off country of South Vietnam to fight communist invaders.

A BLACK CHURCH HAD BEEN BOMBED,

Billy's crusade in the Astrodome in Houston was memorable because it was the first crusade a president attended. President Johnson and his wife, Lady Bird, flew over from their LBJ Ranch west of Austin for the final meeting.

Back in Montreat, Billy's daughter Anne married Danny Lotz. That winter Billy went to South Vietnam. He preached to the soldiers twenty-five times, often combining talents with comedian Bob Hope.

The situation in Vietnam was far worse than Billy had thought. Unless America threw its full might into the war, he saw no way to win and no way to get out. He acted as if he were optimistic, so the troops would not be discouraged. But he left convinced Vietnam was the most unfortunate foreign venture ever in America's long history.

BILLY WENT TO SOUTH VIETNAM.

"THE JOHNSON MEN DO NOT LIVE LONG."

11

In 1967 Billy spent a lot of time with President Johnson. Many times he was a guest at Camp David, the White House, or the LBJ Ranch.

Pressured by President Johnson, Congress had passed many laws giving black Americans justice and equal rights. Yet President Johnson was very unpopular in America because of the war in Vietnam. And the war was crushing him. He took every American death in the war personally.

"The Johnson men do not live long," confided Johnson to Billy. In one very dark mood he told Billy he wanted him to preach at his funeral. "Say something nice about me," he muttered.

In 1968 while Billy was in Australia, America turned topsy-turvy. President Johnson announced he would not run for president again. Days later Martin Luther King Jr. was killed by a sniper.

Things did not improve after Billy returned to America. Robert Kennedy was assassinated in Los Angeles, just as his brother John had been assassinated five years earlier in Dallas.

Billy was heartsick. He said, "America is going through its greatest crisis since the Civil War."

In the election for president, Richard Nixon squeaked out a narrow victory. President-elect Nixon asked Billy to say a prayer at his swearing-in ceremony in January. There was little doubt that President Nixon had a special regard for Billy. Richard Nixon was the first president to have a regular White House church service on Sunday morning. He asked Billy to preach the very first service.

In December 1968 Billy had been called to Walter Reed Hospital in Washington, D.C. Ike was dying. He had asked for Billy. They talked about

HE ASKED BILLY TO PREACH THE VERY FIRST SERVICE.

eternity with God. Weeks later Ike was dead. An older era died with the old peacemaker.

Race and the war in Vietnam were burning issues in America. Billy continued to encourage everyone involved in the racial conflicts to cool off their tempers. He continued to give spiritual support to American troops in Vietnam.

Billy also continued his crusades. President Nixon spoke at Billy's crusade in Knoxville. Billy was delighted. It was so important to have the president openly testify about his faith in God.

"If only I could get President Nixon to call for a national day of repentance like Abraham Lincoln had!" cried Billy.

In 1969, Billy's daughter Bunny married Ted Dienert. Ruth was dealing with a rebellious Franklin, now seventeen. Several times she decided to win him over by showing him what a good sport she was. She hopped on his motorcycle, only to run it over an

PRESIDENT NIXON SPOKE AT BILLY'S CRUSADE IN KNOXVILLE.

embankment once, into a lake once, and into a fence once.

Ruth was never the sophisticated socialite she appeared to be. She was more at home clubbing a rattlesnake on the mountain behind Little Piney Cove than clubbing a golf ball. Billy had always known that and loved her all the more for it.

In October 1971 Charlotte held a Billy Graham Day. President Nixon praised Billy. Billy liked Richard Nixon. He saw a warm side of the president that few people ever saw.

In 1973 Billy's old friend Lyndon Johnson died of a heart attack on almost the same day as the war in Vietnam stopped! It was as if the former president could at last rest in peace. As he'd promised, Billy spoke at the funeral in Texas.

The same year President Johnson found peace, President Nixon found turmoil. Some of his campaign workers had broken into an office of the

PRESIDENT NIXON PRAISED BILLY.

Democratic National Committee at the Watergate Apartments. It seemed trivial at first, but some people thought President Nixon was lying about knowing anything about the incident.

Ever so slowly over the next year the truth crept out: President Nixon had lied, trying to coverup the petty crime. On August 9, 1974, Richard Nixon became the only president in United States history to resign.

Some critics wanted to tar and feather Billy with President Nixon, saying Billy was an insider. The irony was that Billy had known far more about the inner workings of Lyndon Johnson's White House than Richard Nixon's. But as usual, Billy ignored slander and vicious remarks.

The years of 1973 and 1974 were very hard on the Grahams at home, too. Ruth's father, Nelson Bell, passed away. Ruth's mother died shortly after that. Ruth wobbled on crutches at her mother's funeral,

THE YEARS OF 1973 AND 1974 WERE VERY HARD.

recovering from a severe fall she had taken playing with the grandchildren.

Billy's mother was alive but feeble. Psalm 34 comforted her: "The angel of the Lord encampeth round about them that fear him, and delivereth them." She would live to be nearly ninety. At least the Grahams no longer had to worry about Franklin. He had come to his senses and fully accepted Jesus as his Lord.

BGEA had two major successes in 1975 away from the crusade circuit. Billy's book Angels became a best-seller. And World Wide Pictures made its best film ever, The Hiding Place, about the heroic ten Boom family of Holland. The family hid Jews and other refugees during World War II at a heavy price: imprisonment in Nazi death camps. The family's lone survivor of the camps, spunky, eighty-three-year-old Corrie ten Boom, still preached the gospel, living out of a suitcase.

BILLY'S MOTHER WOULD LIVE TO BE NEARLY NINETY.

For several years Billy had known Alex Haraszti, a surgeon from Atlanta. Haraszti had immigrated from Hungary to escape Communism. In 1977 Haraszti shocked Billy by asking "How would you like to hold a full-fledged crusade in Hungary?"

"A crusade for Christ in a communist country? Of course I would!"

"Leave it to me," said Alex Haraszti.

By late 1977 Billy opened his crusade in a church in Budapest, Hungary. The few hundred Hungarians there were not friendly. Yet, as always, Billy's preaching won their hearts. Their hostility turned into anticipation, then love. By the end of ten days, Billy had preached several times—once to a crowd of thirty thousand!

"A CRUSADE FOR CHRIST IN A COMMUNIST COUNTRY?"

BILLY BEGAN WORK ON THE THIRD GREAT GOAL OF HIS LIFE.

12

The Hungarian triumph seemed to break down the barriers to communist countries. The word spread at the highest levels: Billy was not dangerous. He might even satisfy the people's hunger for God—which never seemed to go away.

The next year, 1978, Billy preached in another communist country, Poland. Billy always met with communist officials first. He explained patiently that Christians were good citizens, illustrating with Romans 13 that the Bible instructed Christians to obey authorities. Billy took the officials from the Ten Commandments to Christ's Sermon on the Mount.

Billy began work on the third great goal of his life. The first had been his commitment to preach the gospel of Jesus Christ. The second had been the elimination of racial injustice. The third goal was world peace. And world peace could never be attained without dealing with the communists.

"To reach the center of communism, Russia, would be a real triumph for Christ," Billy prayed.

Once again Alex Haraszti helped bring Billy's prayers to reality. Billy arrived in Moscow in May 1982 to preach the gospel of Jesus Christ!

In September 1984 Billy got his first crusade in Russia. If the trip were not triumphant enough for Billy, there was an added victory. Billy's son Franklin, a newly ordained pastor, preached with him.

All that success was dimmed for Billy by a great personal loss. Grady Wilson passed away in 1987. At the funeral Billy told mourners what a great inspiration Grady had been to him. Billy always regretted how he overshadowed his buddies on the team. Grady had been a fine preacher, and he was the one who loosened up worriers like Lyndon Johnson and

GRADY WILSON PASSED AWAY IN 1987.

Richard Nixon with his barrage of humor.

In America during the 1980s and 1990s, Billy continued city-wide crusades, but more and more he preached on an international scale. Beyond America, the communist world was changing. The Berlin Wall came down.

And Billy achieved another goal: holding a crusade in communist China. He and Ruth, a "daughter of China," got a rousing welcome in the Great Hall of the People in Beijing. From there Billy began a five-city crusade.

In 1989 BGEA launched Mission World. With communications satellites in space circling the globe, a revival could be beamed to many portable receiving stations all around the world.

From London, Billy spoke live to Britain, Ireland, and ten African countries. Delayed broadcasts were received by another twenty-three African countries. In late 1990, Mission World eventually reached

IN 1989 BGEA LAUNCHED MISSION WORLD.

millions in Asia from Billy's live revival in Hong Kong. Some were saying it reached one hundred million viewers!

Communism was unraveling all around the world at an astounding rate. Most shocking of all was the change in Russia. Russians dissolved their communist government in 1991 and replaced it with a democracy.

In 1992 Billy held a city-wide crusade in Moscow. Cliff Barrows could not play the usual music during the altar call. It made the Russians flock to the altar dangerously fast.

"Please walk. Don't run," pleaded Billy. He had never seen such spiritual hunger. The Russians had been denied Christ for seventy-five years!

Over the years Billy had suffered many illnesses: eye problems, kidney stones, hernias, ulcers, tumors, high blood pressure, pneumonia, prostate trouble, and broken ribs. During 1992 his latest affliction was

HE HAD NEVER SEEN SUCH SPIRITUAL HUNGER.

diagnosed: Parkinson's disease. Tiredness as well as tremors in Billy's hands were the obvious signs of this progressive nervous disorder.

"God comes with greater power when we are weak," answered Billy to anyone who implied he should retire. But at seventy-three, Billy not only had nineteen grandchildren, but five great-grandchildren as well.

In March 1993 from Germany, Billy again preached over a satellite network. This time the team emphasized counseling. BGEA focused not so much on how many people they could reach, but on how many people they could reach where counseling was available.

The new direction called for a new name: Global Mission. In 1995, Global Mission was huge. From Puerto Rico, Billy's sermons went to 30 satellites that sent them on to 3,000 sites in 185 countries around the world. One million counselors were waiting to

"GOD COMES WITH GREATER POWER WHEN WE ARE WEAK."

help the new Christians. The effort did not end there. Tapes were to be shown to more and more sites in the months ahead.

The goal was to reach one billion people!

By 1997 Billy had evangelized in city-wide crusades for over fifty years, first in America and then in countries around the world. In moments of exhaustion, Billy thought about retiring.

Only God knew how many people Billy had preached to in one way or another. More than any evangelist in history, he had fulfilled the Great Commission: "Go ye therefore, and teach all nations, baptizing them in the name of the Father, and of the Son, and of the Holy Ghost" (Matthew 28:19).

And yet billions of souls remained to be saved. So, Billy, in failing health, would continue to evangelize. As he had said so many times, "I'll keep opening doors. God will sort it all out."

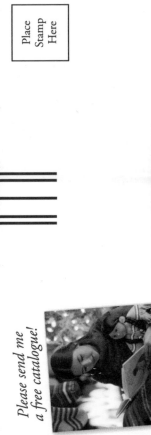

*Please send me
a free catalogue!*

ST4

American Girl®

PO Box 620497
MIDDLETON WI   53562-0497

A free catalogue!

If you or a friend would enjoy receiving
a free American Girl® catalogue,
just mail this card. Or you can call
1-800-845-0005 or visit americangirl.com.

Send me a catalogue:

Name _____ ___/___/___
                                    Girl's birth date

Address _____

City _____ State _____ Zip _____

E-mail *(Fill in to receive updates and Web-exclusive offers.)*

_____

Phone ❏ Home ❏ Work

(___) _____

Parent's signature _____ 18572i

Send my friend a catalogue:

Name _____

Address _____

City _____ State _____ Zip _____ 18580i

"I'LL KEEP OPENING DOORS. GOD WILL SORT IT ALL OUT."

AWESOME BOOKS FOR KIDS!

The Young Reader's Christian Library
Action, Adventure, and Fun Reading!

This series for young readers ages 8 to 12 is action-packed, fast-paced, and Christ-centered! With exciting illustrations on every other page following the text, kids won't be able to put these books down! Over 100 illustrations per book. All books are paperbound. The unique size (4 3/16" x 5 3/8") makes these books easy to take anywhere!

A Great Selection to Satisfy All Kids!

Abraham Lincoln	In His Steps	Prudence of Plymouth
Ben-Hur	Jesus	Plantation
Billy Sunday	Joseph	Robinson Crusoe
Christopher Columbus	Lydia	Roger Williams
Corrie ten Boom	Miriam	Ruth
David Livingstone	Paul	Samuel Morris
Deborah	Peter	The Swiss Family
Elijah	The Pilgrim's Progress	Robinson
Esther	Pocahontas	Taming the Land
Heidi	Pollyanna	Thunder in the Valley
Hudson Taylor		Wagons West